Common Sense

How America Should Be Governed

As always, thanks to God for the gift of writing

To my husband Rodney, for the constant support
and constructive criticism

To my parents, who have made me the outspoken
individual that I am today

To all my readers, if you keep reading, I will keep
writing

Table of Contents

Prayer in Schools

I will be the first to admit that America is the best
country in the world and the only place I would
want to live. However, America has loads of
problems and issues. Most will say that problems
usually start at the top and work down. But that is
not always true. Most problems start small, at the
bottom, and when not handled, they grow in size,
increase, and multiply. Many of America's
problems began over fifty years ago. One of the
biggest changes that began the tear down of our
society began with the removal of prayer in
schools, which is loosely based on the First
Amendment stating that Congress should make no
law that respects the establishment of religion.
Okay, fine. We aren't asking anyone to make a law
concerning it for or against it. But to say that a
child cannot say his/her prayers over their meal in
school or at any other time is just wrong. America
is quickly going to hell in a hand-basket and we

have no one but ourselves to thank for the demise that has become our country. Who is it harming for an individual to quietly say their prayers and give thanks to the only one and true God for the meal that they are about to partake of. If you don't want your child to pray in school, that is your prerogative. Just don't prevent my children from praying. Additionally, when sickness, disease, and death visit your doorstep, no priest, preacher, or bishop should be allowed to visit or pray for you.

We have laws that govern the separation of church and state, and all of them are a load of bull. How can you have a separation of church and state, when for each and every election, local, state, and government, all of the polling places are churches. Am I the only person that has noticed this?

Shorter Work Week

America is a country that works far more than any other country, yet we are no better off. No person should have to work more than a 4 day work week and for no more than 8 hours per day. Our children are suffering because both parents have to work hours upon hours just to make ends meet. Children are left to their own devices, and that is where trouble begins. Parents have no true way of knowing what time their child actually arrives at home, if at all, or if they arrive with someone. Children should be constantly monitored in order to ensure their safety. If families spent more time together, families would be closer and more in touch with their children and with the issues that they may be facing. We cannot expect teachers and principals to catch every oddity that may occur with our children. We are the parents. Therefore, we are the ones ultimately responsible.

All jobs should give each employee time off for sick children, no questions asked, and without them having to bring in a note from a doctor. If my child has the runs all night and is throwing up, why the hell am I going to waste gas and spend money running to the doctor's office, resulting in a co-pay, just for them to tell me that he has a stomach bug, or that he ate something that didn't agree with him. Some things are just common sense. No degree needed. It has been proven that employees who are entrusted with more are more loyal to their employer.

Lock the Doors

As a child, I recall when snacks in vending machines were only 15 cents. I remember when gas was well under $1 per gallon. I even remember when no stores were open on Sunday. Oh, but now, we think it strange if a store is not open. I'm sure I am not the only one who believes that some things were better way back when. No retail store (and that includes you Wal-mart) should be opened past 10 pm. No gas station or convenience store should be opened past midnight. No store, restaurant, or gas station/convenience store should be opened on Sunday. Twenty and thirty years ago, there was far less crime. But the more we have made things and places "convenient" for people, the more we have also opened ourselves up to more crime. The world is filled with evil people. Unfortunately, we cannot get rid of all the evil, but we can certainly circumvent it. You will be surprised how much better people will plan their trips to the store if these new measures are implemented. People are creatures of habit, therefore any new measure implemented will over time be like second nature.

Educate our Children

It is of the utmost importance that our children receive the best possible education that America has to offer. We are at the bottom when it comes to our students in comparison to students from other countries. There should be no cost for a college education for anyone who has graduated from high school on time, with their class, (not a GED or a summer graduation) and who graduated with a grade point average of 3.0 or above. The only cost for each student should be for books. Any student graduating from high school on time with their class should automatically be accepted to any institution of higher learning that they apply to. Having to attain a certain score on the SAT or an ACT for college entry would be no more. If they made the grades and put forth the effort in high school, there is a good chance they will perform the same or better in college.

If that same student decides to further their education even more with graduate school, then they will have to foot the bill themselves. However, if they graduated with a grade point average of 3.7 or higher, then the government will split the cost with them. The portion that the government pays will not have to be paid back.

It Sickens Me

Every time there is a killing in a school, church, or public place, we are quick to say that the person responsible was "sick". Yes, they were sick. Sick with demons... And more than half of them always do the same thing… they kill themselves instead of facing the music, which proves they are punks. These are people with too much time on their hands. Oh, he was sick, he was off his medication, that's why he didn't know what he was doing. If he had no idea what he was doing, then why the hell didn't he go walking inside a police station and start firing in there? Oh, wait, let me, let me tell you… BECAUSE HE KNEW EXACTLY WHAT THE HELL HE WAS DOING.

Too Much Money

America is a country that relishes in sex, lies, and any other bad habit that does nothing for our youth and in no way establishes us as a front runner in the world. We pay celebrities and athletes hundreds of millions of dollars to make us laugh and cheer. Yet, when it comes to the paying of our teachers, who have a hand in the development of our children, we want to pay them pennies. Does anyone not see what is wrong with this picture? Tell me why I should pay someone millions of dollars to run up and down a court chasing a ball and throwing it in a net? Why should I pay someone millions of dollars to learn a script and then watch them play make pretend on the big screen? Why should I pay someone millions to dance on a stage or sing a song to me? Why should I pay someone millions to sit in a chair with a camera in front of them and an audience as they try to tell me how to lose weight or the best gifts to buy this Christmas season? So you see the pattern? It's all centered around entertainment. Americans are willing to pay money just so someone can entertain them. Is there really a need for a single person to net more than one million dollars per year? If America can learn how to share the wealth it will make for a better society and country. There would be less crime and more opportunities, not to mention more equality. Those who are homeless will be given a job and simple housing so that they may get on their feet. Even the bible states that those who do not work will not eat and that the man who does not take care of his family is worse than an infidel. No one should be obligated to feed you when you are more than capable of taking a job and earning an income for you and your family. Be responsible.

Focus on America

Every year we lend money to other nations. How exactly are we able to that when we are operating in the red? If I am in debt, how the hell am I able to loan you money? That makes zero sense. I recently read an article in a Florida newspaper which stated that Florida was going in to 2013 with a surplus of $238 million. Yet, in the very next sentence, it clearly stated that those in charge of that money were working on a budget that would be in the billions. What the hell? Did we really vote total idiots into office? It appears that those who have more education are total fools when it comes to common sense. Not only does it seem that way, it is that way, and so, common sense, apparently isn't so very common anymore.

America spends entirely too much time worrying about other nations instead of worrying about itself. Until we can get to the point where we focus on just America and taking care of the people of this country, we will keep digging ourselves into a deeper hole. Would it make any sense for me to walk next door to my neighbor's house and cook them dinner when I haven't even cooked dinner for my own household? Every month there is a different celebrity on television begging those of us who make considerably less than they to send other countries money to feed the little child with the big stomach from Africa.

If I am a celebrity making millions per year, per movie, per game, per episode, then why the hell am I begging someone who makes less than me? Why am I asking "common folk" to send their hard earned money to another country when I can send $1 million dollars myself and write it off on my taxes? If common people would just take the time to think they would realize what I have realized all along… celebrities care nothing about you. They have no idea who you are. All they want is for you to watch their show, take in their movie, and come to their game. Yet when you encounter that very same celebrity on the street and you approach them, they either ignore you, or have their people remove you from their circle. Again, this is the same celebrity who said it's all about the fans. Total bullshit. And when it's all said and done, they will be even richer and you, Mr. and Mrs. Common Folk will still be the same poor/middle class person you always have been. There are plenty of homeless and down and out people right here in America. Why not try taking care of them first before hopping a plane to some third world country to help a people who God has plainly stated in His word are cursed. If God curses someone, please tell me how you think you can help them. If I side with someone that God is against, then I also position myself against God. Is that a fight that I really want to be in? It's time to wake up.

Too Much Too Soon

Time has proven that the more money a person makes, the more ways they come up with to waste it on frivolous items, especially if they are under the age of 35 years. Most of the problems in Hollywood with young celebrities stem from them making too much money too soon. If you have never had millions of dollars in your sole possession all at once, then how will you know how to handle it, except you surround yourself with the right type of people.

It used to be surprising, but it no longer is, to see someone who once made millions a year and yet they are now poor and working alongside everyday people. It's all because they got too much too soon and could not handle it. They were not mature. The amount of money a person makes should be based on #1: How old you are and #2: What career you are in.

Example: If I am 16 years old and am the leading actress in a movie, then I should be making no more than #1: twice my age, which would be $32,000 per movie and #2: based on my career as an actress, no more than 5% of what the movie grosses. So if I happen to be in a movie that brings in $20 million, then I will gross $1 millions for that particular movie. Likewise, if the movie does not so great and brings in only $1 million, then I will only gross $50k, which would still be a pretty damn good payday for a 16 year old.

Out of the Sky

America has spent millions upon millions of dollars towards NASA and the space shuttle. This has been a total waste of time, space (no pun intended), energy, and money. The entire operation was totally pointless. Some will say well, we had a man walk on the moon, and we discovered another planet or some more stars. Again, what for? Wasted time is what it was and has always been. The space shuttle program, though no one will publicly admit it, is the biggest leach in our government. This is where the bulk of our deficit has derived from. And what do we have to show for it? Not a damn thing. No man will ever live on the moon or any other planet. God created Earth as man's residence. What they haven't told you is that in addition to discovering and having a closer look at planets in hopes that you will find other life, inwardly they are hoping that man can one day live in space. Sorry rich man and rich woman, that just isn't happening. Not in this lifetime or the next one. However, if you are insistent on trying anyway, then everyone who supports it and/or wants to live there, should be loaded onto one space shuttle and flown into space. Once there, the space shuttle will disintegrate, leaving their bodies floating in the air. Hope they enjoy the experience of their new residence.

Billions to Banks

When banks began to crumble, many blamed the mortgage lenders stating that they made loans to people who could not afford it. And yes, that could very well be true. However, no one made them sign on the dotted line. Everyone has a brain, or at least they should, though many don't bother to exercise it. Everyone knows whether or not they can afford something. The people who apply for and purchase homes are supposed to be adults. The key word here is SUPPOSED. If you bought a house under false pretenses knowing good and hell well that you could not afford it, then you need to be homeless. It's time out for everyone else coming to the rescue of stupid people. I don't blame the banks. I blame the people. Yet on the other side of that coin, banks should not expect payment from someone whom they knew full well could not afford the payments. If you give someone money, knowing that there is only a small chance of them repaying it, then you need to lose out.

The federal government came to the rescue of many banks. And what for? Why didn't the government come to the rescue of the people? Instead of the millions that was given to banks, that money should have been distributed across America to households. If households have more money, they will spend more money, thus reviving the economy. Giving the banks money will not make the economy grow, especially when banks are now refusing to lend to everyday people. The government rescued the banks and many of them have already begun to default on those loans, yet they have no mercy on the homeowners who defaulted on their loans. Does anyone see a pattern here, besides me?

Pack 'Em In

Has anyone noticed that whether you're buying a million dollar home or not, all homes are sandwiched together onto one lot? It's because of greed. Developers want to pack as many homes onto one lot as they possibly can and still charge far more than what they are worth, as homes are made with far cheaper material now than they were fifty years ago. Who else agrees that there should only be one house per lot with each lot being a minimum of one acre. If children have more room to run and play, they will spend less time in front of the tube or looking at a computer. Staring at any type of screen requires no thought process, and therefore is a waste of time.

The criteria and process for purchasing a home or vehicle should and can be made a lot simpler. Just the other day my husband and I took my Armada to the Nissan dealership to have some work done to it. As we pulled into the dealership, we saw the vultures waiting. There had to be at least eight salesman standing in front of the door that led inside. As my husband circled for a park, I saw a guy leave the pack and begin walking towards our vehicle. Is this guy really following us I thought? We parked and as soon as my husband opened his door to get out, the salesman was right there. I mean literally right there. I was like, WTF! We can't even get out of our vehicles without literally being harassed. Thank God we were not there to purchase. Who knows what would have happened next. My husband being the man that he is told the guy to get lost. I almost cracked a rib from laughter. But it amazes me how it takes them an hour or more just to run your credit, print out paperwork for car buyers to sign, to have the vehicle detailed , and hand you the damn keys.

I recall the closing process of our first home to be much shorter than the process of buying a car, and a home costs a hell of a lot more and doesn't depreciate. I realize that there is certain criteria that has to be met when buying either. I am aware that a person's credit score should be at least 620 to buy a home and at least 650 to buy a car, that is, without having to put down $5k or more, which in itself, is useless because each grand that is put down only takes ten dollars off the monthly payment. So when they try to feed you that crap about you needing to put down "x" amount of dollars in order to qualify is a load of crap. Either I qualify or I don't. Besides, my being able to save up $5k for a down payment, in no way proves that I will be able to make the monthly payment. Am I the only person who realizes this? The credit score for buying a car should be considerably lower than the score needed to buy a home. Furthermore, each dealership should only pull the score from the credit reporting agency closest to where you live. Since I live in Florida, only my Equifax score should be used, although time has proven that they are slow to remove errors but quick to add something negative. Additionally, a person's income should have a bigger weight than their credit score when qualifying for either.

To Serve & Protect

When it comes to our policemen and policewoman who are supposed to protect us, many of the times, it's them who are abusing their power. Not a week goes by that I don't see a cop turn on his sirens and flashing light only to run through an intersection just to get to McDonald's to order a Value Meal. We see cops use excessive force time and time again. There is still much hatred towards minorities and it shows every day. Any cop caught breaking the law should immediately lose his job. No questions asked. No more paid time off while we try to figure out if you did it or not. But to allow him/her to remain in their same field, their new career should be that of a security guard (and one that does not carry a firearm).

Sir, Yes Sir!

Men and women who enter the military will no
longer get a bunch of free rides. The same
opportunities will be available to them as to other
men and women who go on to college after high
school, which I stated previously. No more special
parades or free meals on Veteran's Day. Why the
special treatment? You made the decision to enter
the military. It's the job you chose. We don't
parade our nurses and doctors through the streets
or give them special days and they save hundreds
of lives every day. No one pats them on the back
or gives them a leg up to the better paying jobs. So
what makes you so special? Yes, you go to other
countries and fight and defend. But most of the
fighting has been for others, not for America. And
even when the fighting is for America, it is still
YOUR CHOICE to sign up for the military. So
stop expecting special perks from the world. I am
an author and an editor, but I don't expect to be

published in every newspaper. I don't expect to have a contract with every publishing house or receive newspapers and magazines at no cost to me. Do I receive a new laptop each year from Best Buy as a perk for doing my job? Nope.

Unequally Balanced

Our judicial system is broken. We have stupid ass lawyers who will knowingly defend someone whom they know full well have either murdered, molested, raped, or killed someone. Why? Because they have no morals. They have no conscience. All they want is a big payday or publicity. Lawyers who defend a known murderer, rapist, molester, or killer, and the defendant ends up going scot free, immediately following the ruling, the attorney(s) should be made to house the known criminal in their home with their family. If people are made to deal with the crappy choices they make, over time, they will make better choices and become a better person. But if no one ever has to own up and pay for their mistakes, then they will never learn, progress, and become a better person.

Our legal system still has a lot of kinks in it that need to be worked out. For example, no case should go to trial without all the evidence being presented. To have a trial and hold back some of the evidence is totally unfair. If the accused is to have due process and a truly fair trial, then all evidence should be viewed and all evidence should be presented.

Stop the Bleeding

We have so many people who are on welfare for one reason or another. I've know people who have received assistance and both adults have full time jobs. So many people take advantage of the system. Many times those who need it most are turned down unnecessarily. Its disgusts me when I see women who have not one, not two, but three, four, five, sometimes more children, and its not always African-Americans. Many are Caucasians. Many are Latinos. They just keep lying on their backs, spreading their legs, and pushing kids out one after another. There are many receiving assistance who are able to work, but are too lazy to keep a job. If you need assistance, you should be able to receive assistance for up to two years. During which time, you need to show record of your either working at least part-time or seeking work. Once you receive assistance for you and your one child, should you have another child within that initial two year period, your benefits will immediately cease. If you have the time and energy to make another child, then you should be able to work full time to bring in the necessary income to provide for you and your family. It should not be the government's job to take care of you just because you made the decision to keep popping out kids or stand on a corner and not work.

Medicare/Social Security

We are entering a time in which our Medicare laws
are changing. The unfortunate part is that our
parents and grandparents who have worked their
fingers to the bone and are now ready to retire are
not receiving or will not receive the adequate
income necessary to live a life of quality through
social security. No one will ever come forward to
admit this, but I am sure some of the monies that
has been set aside in social security has been
tapped into a time or two, and that's just not right,
nor is it fair. The Medicare laws should be
rewritten so that seniors are in a better position to
receive medical treatment and their prescriptions.
They should not have to pay any sort of co-pay
when seeing their primary doctor, for whatever
reason. All the monies that were taken out of each
person's paycheck should be made available to
them upon them reaching the age of 62 years and
spread out over the next twenty years. Should that

person be diagnosed with a terminally ill condition, then all monies they paid in social security will be paid in one lump sum, if they so desire. When seeing their primary care physicians, seniors should not have any type of co-pay. When seeing a specialist or eye doctor, their co-pay should not exceed ten dollars. If they are in need of eyeglasses, they should receive one pair of glasses per year and one eye exam at no cost. They should be able to visit any optometrist they desire, and that office will receive a tax credit of $200 per senior.

You Were Not Born That Way

I realize that the subject of gays/lesbians is a touchy one with a lot of people. People are going to do what they want regardless. However, only a union between a man and woman should be recognized as legal. Not two men. Not two women. If someone still chooses to have this type of immoral relationship, yes I said it. Immoral, because anything not moral is immoral. Anything not right is wrong. Its time we stop accepting any and every behavior as being okay and "different". It's time we stop tip toeing around people and certain words because we don't want to hurt someone's feelings. As long as you live, and even after you die, there will always be someone talking about you. So grow up and get over it. Man up men! Women, put on your big girl panties! God gave man woman so that he would not be alone. He didn't give man another man, nor did he make two women to live together and be a family. I know it sounds harsh. But if we can tell a woman when she can and cannot have an abortion, then we should have no problem with this. And while we are on the subject, no abortion should be allowed unless the woman has been raped or molested, not just because "someone got caught up in the moment" and now realize that they don't want to be parents. Be responsible. Wear a damn condom and take birth control, or better yet, wait until you're married. Same sex relationships should not be allowed to adopt or have any children as all it does is confuses the child. Children have enough to cope with growing up without us adults adding anything else to the mix. It's time out for all the bullshit. Just be real with yourself. Can two men shoving their penises into each other's ass produce a child? Nope. Can two women rubbing their clitorises together bring about a child? Hell no. And there is a reason why. Believe it or not God is pretty damn smart. He knew exactly what He was doing. No one is born gay. Sexual orientation is a decision. Being born a certain race is not.

'Til Death Do You Part

Every year we have hundreds of thousands of marriages that end in divorce. Why? Because most people marry for the wrong reasons. You cannot just marry for love anymore. And you certainly better not marry for money. If a person's reason for marrying someone else is unjust, the marriage will always either fail or be a total headache. And who may I ask wants to voluntarily live with a headache. A man and a woman should only be allowed to marry once they have met with their priest/pastor and have reached the age of 27 years for a woman and 30 years for a man, as men tend to mature at a much slower rate than women. Both parties should be required to have completed college and to be working full time. Once married, no children should be had until they have been married for at least 5 years. This will give them time to do things together and grow stronger and closer as a couple, prior to bringing another person into the relationship. Contrary to what many may believe, having a child will not make a relationship stronger. If anything, it will make the relationship that much harder. Besides that, why would you want to put that type of responsibility on a child anyway?

You Can't Win If You Don't Play

Each state should be required to have a lottery. Yes, there are a good portion of people who feel the lottery is a waste. Usually, those are the folk who don't have a damn thing and who live a depressing life. It's those who know nothing about handling money and who are total pessimists. They live a life of negativity and want you to do the same. Some say it's throwing away money. Hell, what do you call eating everyday? You eat, then you shit it out. What is it called? Your body getting rid of waste. You buy gas to put in your vehicle week after week, and your vehicle burns it out, and then you do it all over again. Everything can be looked at as being a waste if you want to get technical about it. But if you are the small minority of people who not only have a brain, but actually use it, you will agree with me. A portion of all the proceeds from each state's lottery should go towards the educational fund that helps cover the cost of college as well as primary education for that particular state. For each jackpot, for whatever game, if it exceeds one million dollars, then that jackpot will have the same number of winners. For example, the Powerball starts at forty million dollars each week, so there should be 40 different sets of numbers drawn. This way, the wealth is shared equally among everyone. No one shall receive a lump sum. There will be no cash option for anyone, except, and only in cases in which the recipient is 60 years of age or older. It baffles me as to why someone HAS TO HAVE the lump sum when they have been surviving on less than $40k per year all their lives. But now, all of a sudden, they need the big payout. StuPid with a capital "P" is what it is called. These are the people that are out of control. These are the people that you read about in the newspaper, who one year later are totally broke and now wish they had never won the lottery. Too bad they don't realize that the lottery isn't the problem, they are.

www.ingramcontent.com/pod-product-compliance
Lightning Source LLC
Chambersburg PA
CBHW071730170526
45165CB00005B/2223